100 Easy Smoothie Recipes for Kids

by Debbie Madson

www.kids-cooking-activities.com

Images from Bigstockphoto
Many thanks to our Kids-Cooking-Activities readers for contributing their favorite smoothie recipes for this collaboration cookbook.

About the Author

Debbie Madson is a Web Publisher and Author for children. She has several learning kids websites including:

www.kids-cooking-activities.com
www.kids-sewing-projects.com
www.teaching-kids-money-skills.com

As well as teaching products to aid in these subjects through her websites and TeachersPayTeachers store.
http://www.teacherspayteachers.com/Store/Debbie-Madson

She has many Kindle ebooks for kids fun and entertainment. Debbie also has three kids who are great for helping and contributing to her projects.

Disclaimer and Terms of Use: Effort has been made to ensure that the information in this book is accurate and complete, however, the author and the publisher do not warrant the accuracy of the information, text and graphics contained within the book due to the rapidly changing nature of science, research, known and unknown facts and internet. The Author and the publisher do not hold any responsibility for errors, omissions or contrary interpretation of the subject matter herein. This book is presented solely for motivational and informational purposes only.

Smoothie Recipes for Kids-Why they're great!

Smoothies are an ideal snack for growing kids. In our world of quick, unhealthy snack solutions, it can be hard to make sure your children are getting all the nutrients they need. Add to this the fact that kids are often put off vegetables and fruit because these foods don't have the advertising dollars behind them as certain brands of hamburgers and sugar-loaded cereals. So it can be hard to even persuade your kids to polish off the vegetables on their plate or eat the apple you put in their lunch box.

Smoothies eliminate some of these problems because you don't have to convince the kids to eat anything. If a smoothie tastes good with oranges or strawberries, you can add a stick of celery or two and half the time kids won't even notice the difference. It's a good way to sneak a few extra nutrients into their diet "under the radar."

But ultimately, you want your kids to be in on what goes in their smoothies and start making their own. In this way smoothies can become a great nutritional teaching tool as kids learn that healthy snacks can also taste great.

How to Get Your Kids Involved

Kids are always more likely to eat something healthy if they have a hand in preparing it, and that preparation is fun. So one of the keys to getting kids interested in making smoothies is making the whole process exciting and fun.

One important tip is to keep the recipes simple at first. The easier a smoothie is to make, the faster a kid can pick up the process– and often just being able to do it will inspire your child's enthusiasm. Obviously the younger the child the more help and supervision they will need, but you can let them do things like putting the fruit in the blender and pushing the blend button.

Also, don't be too restrictive on the ingredients you allow in smoothies for kids. You should try to make them healthy, but there's nothing wrong with a dollop of ice cream or some chocolate sprinkles here and there. Just make sure the smoothies lean more towards the healthy ingredients, rather than becoming just another fatty, sugary snack.

When it comes time to make a smoothie, make sure you talk it up. Be excited about it yourself and your kids will follow suit. Try to use different variations when it comes to recipes, and be prepared to experiment with some out-of-the-box food combinations. Of course, with that in mind, you can always bribe a reluctant kid by adding a bit of their favorite food – a dollop of peanut butter can be a great secret weapon.

Great ideas for Simple Smoothie Recipes

Add cream of coconut to a recipe.

Experiment with different juices including vegetable juices.

Try adding a handful of carrots or celery to the smoothie recipe. Once it is blended nobody will know it is an extra healthy smoothie.

Add up to 1 tablespoon sugar or honey for a sweeter flavor.

Add oat bran, almonds or wheat germ for an extra burst of nutrition.

If using canned fruit include the juice for extra flavor.

Add 1 tablespoon peanut butter to your smoothie recipe.

Substitute milk for juice or juice for the milk in any recipe.

To make any simple smoothie recipe thinner add more juice or milk. To make any simple smoothie recipe thicker add more fruit.

Simple Smoothie Tips

I wanted to comment on smoothies. They are so nutritious and fun to make. In a blender, I use oranges, apples, pineapple, bananas and blueberries or strawberries and blend them together.

One additional suggestion: Throw in some carrots, or celery or some other veggies and blend in with the fruits. It doesn't change the taste, just the color and children get their fruits and vegetables all at once. St. Patrick's Day is ideal for green smoothies. Just add celery, spinach or cabbage.

Smoothies are also great for kids to make if they are younger they can easily add the ingredients to the blender and turn on the button with an adult supervising.

Contents

Smoothie Recipes for Kids-Why they're great! 3

How to Get Your Kids Involved 4

Great ideas for Simple Smoothie Recipes........................5

    Simple Smoothie Tips 6

Strawberry Smoothies 13

    Really Simple Strawberry and Banana Smoothie.................13

    Easy & Tasty Strawberry 13

    Strawberry Ice Smoothie 14

    Layered Strawberry Banana Smoothie 14

    Cucumber Strawberry..................................15

    Strawberry Banana Twist..................................15

    Strawberry Sensation..................................15

    Mummy's Berry and Banana whirl..........................16

Orange Smoothies 17

    Strawberry Orange 17

    Sunrise Smoothie 17

    Ornanaberry 18

    Orange Sunrise Smoothie 18

    Orange Julius..................................19

    Apple Orange Banana Smoothie..........................19

    Citrus Smoothie 19

Banana Smoothies 20

    Banana Buzz Smoothie 20

    Strawberry Banana Protein Smoothie 20

The Berry-Bonanza Smoothie 21

Banana Heaven 21

Banana Smoothie 21

Easy Peasy Banana Squeeze 22

Banana Protein 22

New York Style Banana Smoothie..............................22

Mostly, Banana Smoothie...23

Banana Peach smoothie 23

Mixed Fruits Smoothie...24

The Fruity Samba! 24

Berry Banana Pineapple...24

Fruitie Tootie Smoothie!..24

Fruit Salad Smoothie...25

The Smoothie Mix...25

Carrot Smoothie 26

Yummy fruit smoothie with a secret 26

Green Smoothies 27

Mango Smoothies 28

Mango and Strawberries Smoothie 28

Mango Smoothie 28

Mango, Coconut, and Passion Fruit Shake................28

Mango Tropical 29

Mawi Delisiouso..30

Mango Smoothie 30

Mango Banana Coconut 30

Watermelon Smoothies..31

Summer Smoothie 31

Watermelon Smoothie 31

Peach Smoothies 32

Peach Banana Fizz Smoothie 32

Strawberry Peach Swizzle 32

Peach Banana Berry...32

Fruit Smoothie 33

Blueberry Smoothies 34

Blueberry Strawberry...34

Rainbow Smoothie 34

Sherbet Berry 34

Super Berry Smoothie 35

Fruit Craze Smoothie 35

Strawberry & Blueberry Deluxe Smoothie...........................36

Purple Tummy Yummy..36

Apple Smoothies..37

Apple and Ice 37

Apple Orange Smoothie..37

Simple Banana and Apple Blast 38

Healthy Fruit Smoothie Blend.....................................38

Grape Smoothie...39

Grape and Strawberry...39

Grape Orange..39

Coconut Smoothies...40

Jungle Smoothie..40

Coconut Smoothie 40

Hawaii Coconut and Mango Smoothie 40

Pincocoaya 41

Raspberry Smoothie 42

Banana Berry 42

Super Berry Smoothie 42

Mixed Berry 42

Banana Berry 42

Very Berry 43

Kiwi Smoothies 44

Raspberry and Kiwi 44

Kiwi Strawberry Smoothie 44

Strawberry Kiwi..44

Fruit Blend Smoothie 45

Pineapple Smoothie...46

Tutti Frutti Smoothie 46

Strawberry and "Pinana" Swoosh 46

Pineapple Strawberry Banana 46

Banana Pineapple 47

Apple Berry Pine Nana 47

Banana, Coconut, and Pineapple 47

Hawaiian Smoothie 48

Blackberry Smoothie 49

Berry Dream 49

Berry Yogurt Smoothie 49

Moolicious Berry Smoothie 50

Berry Blast 50

Yumberry smoothie 50

Dessert Smoothies 51

Chocolate Smoothie 51

Strawberry Banana Blitz 51

Lemonade smoothie 51

Banana Chocolate Smoothie 51

Jell-O Berry Smoothie 52

Banana Chocolate 52

Banana Surprise 52

Banana Nesquick Smoothie 53

Pumpkin Milkshake 53

Fruit Galore Smoothie 53

Orange Milkshake 54

Peanut Butter Smoothies 55

Peanut Butter and Chocolate Smoothie 55

Elvis Smoothie 55

Peanut Butter Banana 55

Chocolate Drizzle 56

Peanut Butter Banana Smoothie 56

Strawberry Smoothies

Really Simple Strawberry and Banana Smoothie

One chopped ripe banana
Strawberry yogurt (the regular little cups bought in the stores)
Blend until the right thickness.
One banana and one strawberry yogurt equals a half a cup (or a regular kids cup.)

Easy & Tasty Strawberry

1 banana
1/2 cup strawberries
3/4 cup milk
2 tablespoon sugar
8 ice cubes
Blend all in blender until ice cubes are smooth.

Strawberry Ice Smoothie

by Cydney (IL)
1 cup strawberries
1 cup low fat milk
1/2 cup vanilla yogurt
1 cup ice
Blend all in blender on high or until smooth.

Layered Strawberry Banana Smoothie

by Haleh
1 apple
1 banana
1/2 Cup strawberries
1 Cup milk
4 tablespoons plain yogurt
Instructions:
Put all the ingredients in the blender and blend it all
together for about 1 minute, pour it in a glass and decorate
it if you want.
Decorating materials:
1 strawberry
gummy bears (optional)
chocolate chips
whipped cream (chocolate or vanilla)
Decorating instructions:
Pour half of the smoothie in your glass, put a layer of
whipped cream, chocolate chips and gummy bears and pour
the rest of the smoothie on top! then cut the strawberry in
tiny pieces and put it on top followed by another layer of
whipped cream!

Cucumber Strawberry

1 cucumber, peeled and sliced
5-6 strawberries
Blend all together.

Strawberry Banana Twist

by Andrea(United States)
1/2 Banana
1 cup strawberries
Flax seed (optional)
1 cup plain/vanilla yogurt
4 ice cubes
1/4-1/2 can frozen fruit juice (optional)
2 tbsp water
Cut up all fruits and put all ingredients in blender. Blend until smooth. Serves 2-3

Strawberry Sensation

by Andrea (Canada)
Handful of Strawberries (frozen or fresh)
A scoop of Frozen fat free yogurt
2 splashes of guava juice
3 ice cubes
Blend until all ingredients are mixed.

Mummy's Berry and Banana whirl

by Emily (England)
1/2 Cup of fresh strawberries
1/2 Cup of fresh raspberries
1/2 a banana
a teaspoon of apple juice
Put all ingredients in blender and blend until smooth. Fill
2/3 of a glass with ice and pour the smoothie into the glass.
Serve with a straw and a slice of strawberry.

Orange Smoothies

Strawberry Orange

1 cup of strawberries (frozen is best)
1 cup of crushed ice
1 cup of Orange juice or 2 oranges peeled and sectioned
2 containers of any yogurt
Mix in blender until smooth!

Sunrise Smoothie

by Leigh Ann
1/2 Cup orange juice Fruity Sunrise
1/2 Cup peach juice
2 Tablespoons Maraschino cherry juice
5 Maraschino cherries
Mix orange juice and peach juice. Top with cherry juice,
allowing it to blend in slowly making it look like a sunrise.
Drop in Maraschino cherries and serve.

Ornanaberry

by Ciara (Las Vegas)
1 Cup of orange juice
1 Cup strawberry yogurt (or other type of fruit yogurt)
1 banana (diced or sliced)
1/4 Cup of blueberries
4 ice cubes
1/2 Cup of milk
1 teaspoon of vanilla
Blend together.

Orange Sunrise Smoothie

by Ashley (California)
1 can of pineapple slices
1 cup of orange juice
1 whole banana
1/2 cup of %2 low-fat milk
1 cup of ice
Put the pineapple slices, orange juice, banana, and milk all together into the blender. Mix them up and one at a time add the ice cubes through the blender tube.

Orange Julius

6oz. orange juice concentrate
2 cups milk
1/4 Cup sugar
2 teaspoons vanilla
5 ice cubes
Blend together until ice is crushed.

Apple Orange Banana Smoothie

by Jennifer (Utah)
1 Apple peeled and cut into slices
1 Orange peeled with pulp off and sectioned
1 Banana peeled and cut into slices
Ice cubes (as many as it takes or as many as you want)
1 Cup of orange juice
Now what you want to do is add everything together into the blender. Then you want to mix it all. Make sure that you mix it until it is how you want it or until it is smooth. Then you can do what I like to do and put it in a fancy cup with a drink umbrella and treat your children like royalty. I know that my children love it and they tell me that it feels like their in Hawaii. Enjoy!

Citrus Smoothie

2 T. lime juice
1 orange (or tangerine) peeled
2 T. lemon juice
2 Cups orange juice
8 oz. yogurt any flavor or plain
Feel free to add any strawberries, bananas, apples or any other fruit for flavor
Blend until smooth.

Banana Smoothies

Banana Buzz Smoothie

by Branko(Australia)
2 halved bananas
1 teaspoon of honey (optional)
5-8 blocks of ice
1/2 cup of milk
Blend until smooth.

Strawberry Banana Protein Smoothie

1-2 Bananas
4 strawberries
1 small container of vanilla yogurt
1 Big Cup Of Ice
A Little Dash Of Protein Powder
Blend until smooth.

The Berry-Bonanza Smoothie

1 cup of milk
2 cups frozen fruit
1 sliced banana
1 Cup vanilla yogurt
Blend until smooth.

Banana Heaven

by Kimberley (England)
3 bananas chopped
1-2 Cups of milk
1 Cup of yogurt any flavor
1/2 cup of ice cubes
Blend all together.

Banana Smoothie

by Hallie (OH)
1 banana chopped
1/2 cup V-8 fruit juice any flavor
Blend together.

Easy Peasy Banana Squeeze

by Chloe (newcastle)
2 Bananas
3 scoops of banana/vanilla ice cream or yogurt
1 Cup of milk.
Blend for 1 minute for perfect results and serve in glass with real dairy cream squirted on in a spiral, it is a good idea to add a slice of banana on top. For my kids as a little treat I often sprinkle hundreds and thousands/ sprinkles on top.

Banana Protein

by Nicole (MN)
1 banana (cut up)
2 Tablespoons sugar
1/2 Cup milk
1 oz. protein powder
Mix in blender.

New York Style Banana Smoothie

1-5 bananas
3 tablespoons of orange juice
1/2 Cup ice cubes
1 Cup yogurt
Mix ingredients together in a blender and blend until completely smooth

Mostly, Banana Smoothie

3-5 Bananas
1/2 T. of Honey
1/2 Cup of almond (to make it crunchy),
1 Cup of milk,
3-4 ice cubes
Blend until smooth.

Banana Peach smoothie

by Garett & Shelby (N.M)
First, you will need a banana, milk, and a peach yogurt. Cut up the banana and put it in the blender along with peach yogurt and 1 cup of milk then blend it until creamy.

Mixed Fruits Smoothie

The Fruity Samba!

by Chrystyna (Canada)
12 Strawberries
1 Nectarine or peach
1/4 Cup plain yogurt
1/4 Cup or less sugar
A splash of lemon juice (optional)
Blend and enjoy!!

Berry Banana Pineapple

1 medium banana
a handful blueberries
5 pineapple slices
2-5 ice cubes
Blend until smooth.

Fruitie Tootie Smoothie!

by Danii
1 Banana peeled
1 orange peeled
6 frozen strawberries
1 1/2 cups of orange juice
Blend until smooth.

Fruit Salad Smoothie

by sarah
1 small tin fruit salad (and juice too)
1 small tub yogurt
hand full of ice cubes
Just put it all and the blender and enjoy.
Place a dollop of whip cream on top of every individual smoothie!

The Smoothie Mix

Pour a little bit of orange juice and milk in a blender.
Next throw in some strawberries or other frozen fruit. Then any type of yogurt, I put in blueberry yogurt. Then put some ice cubes in for thickness.

Carrot Smoothie

Yummy fruit smoothie with a secret

by Matilda (South Africa)
This is very nice and my kids absolutely love this!
1 banana, cut in pieces
4-5 strawberries
handful of grapes
1 pear sliced
1/2 Cup Mango juice or other tropical flavor
3-4 slices of Pineapple
2 Carrots, cut in chunks (secret ingredient)
5-6 ice cubes
Start with the juice and carrots and make sure the carrots are blended very finely. Thereafter you can add the other fruit and the ice. This is absolutely delicious.

Green Smoothies

by Mrs. Monasterski's Class (MI)
In a blender add:
9 grapes
2 large pieces of honey dew, chopped
1 green apple, chopped
8 slices of frozen peaches
1 Cup spinach
4 crowns of broccoli
1 Cup milk
1 serving of vanilla protein powder
Add all ingredients in the blender and put blender on chop speed. When chopped you can change it to puree or blend speed until smooth. Add ice if you want. Put into a tall glass and enjoy your healthy green drink!

Mango Smoothies

Mango and Strawberries Smoothie

by Ashleigh (Australia)
1 Cup of mango slices
4 large strawberries
1 scoop of strawberry yogurt
1 Cup of orange juice
10 ice cubes
Put into a blender and blend until smooth

Mango Smoothie

2 1/2 cups of Mango Juice
1 Cup of Vanilla yogurt or plain
1 Sliced Banana
Blend all ingredients together.

Mango, Coconut, and Passion Fruit Shake

by Alice(Georgia)
1 large mango peeled, or 1 1/4 cups of mango puree
6 large passion fruit, or 2/3 cup of passion fruit juice
3/4 cup of coconut milk
12 ice cubes
Instructions:
Cut the mango flesh away from the pit. Coarsely chop the
flesh and put into a blender. Cut the passion fruit in half
and scoop the seeds into a strainer set over a bowl. Use a
spoon to press down the seeds and extract all the juice. Add
the juice, coconut milk, and ice cubes to the
blender and puree until smooth.

Mango Tropical

by Jessica (CA)
2 sliced and peeled bananas
1 half can of dole pineapple
1 1/2 Cups of strawberry
1-2 bananas
half a mango
1-2 scoops coconut ice cream or yogurt
Blend until smooth

Mawi Delisiouso

by Alexa (Michigan)
2 kiwis, peeled and cut in half
1 mango, peeled and cut in pieces
1 1/2 Cup of orange juice
1 Cup of ice or more if you want
First put in the mango and kiwis and orange juice. When all of that is blended, put in the ice. Blend until smooth

Mango Smoothie

3 scoops of mango sorbet
1 Cup of mango yogurt
1/2 Cup milk
1 Cup crushed ice cubes
1 banana (sliced)
Mix in a blender until smooth.

Mango Banana Coconut

by Hannah (OR)
2 soft mangoes, peeled and cut in pieces
1 Cup of milk
2 bananas, cut in slices
1/2 Cup of strawberries
1/4 Cup coconut (optional)
Add to blender and mix till smooth

Watermelon Smoothies

Summer Smoothie

by Matilda (South Africa)
1 mango, peeled and cut in pieces
2 Cups watermelon cut in pieces
1 orange peeled and sectioned
1 carrot, peeled and cut in slices
4-5 ice cubes
Blend all together and enjoy.

Watermelon Smoothie

by Shanna And Kaitlynn (WI)
6 or so pieces, cut up cantaloupe
10 or so frozen strawberries
2 pinches of sugar
4 medium sized watermelon chunks
1/2 Cup of regular pineapple juice
1/2 Cup of vanilla yogurt
Blend until smooth.

Peach Smoothies

Peach Banana Fizz Smoothie

by Julie and Phil
1 Nectarine or peach, cut in slices
1 Peach flavored yogurt
1 Plum, cut in half
2 tablespoons of Sugar (optional)
1 teaspoon of Cinnamon
1 3/4 cups of Milk
5 Ice cubes
2 Bananas
Blend together until smooth!

Strawberry Peach Swizzle

by Katie (Ireland)
1 Cup of strawberries
1/2 Cup of yogurt, any flavor or plain
1/2 Cup of chopped banana
1 sliced peach
1 Cup of ice cubes
1 Cup of orange juice
1/2 Cup of strawberry juice
Blend all together.

Peach Banana Berry

by Savanna (usa)
5 strawberries
4 peaches, cut in slices
2 bananas, cut in slices
2 Tbsp. of honey

1 1/4 Cup milk
6 ice cubes
Blend all together.

Fruit Smoothie

by taylor (MO)
2 Cups of peach slices
1 Cup of apricot slices
1 Cup of fruit cocktail
1/2 Cup of milk
4-5 ice cubes
Blend in blender until liquid and no more ice chunks.

Blueberry Smoothies

Blueberry Strawberry

1/2 Cup ice cubes
1/2 Cup orange juice
1/2 Cup strawberries
1/2 Cup blueberries
Add all ingredients to blender and blend until ice cubes are crushed.

Rainbow Smoothie

by Ashley (Georgia)
1/2 Cup orange juice
1 Cup mixed raspberries or berry mixture
1/2 Cup milk
1/2 Cup crushed ice
1 Cup yogurt
1 banana
Blend together.

Sherbet Berry

by Abby (Wisconsin)
1 1/2 Cups Blueberries
As much as you need/want of Orange Sherbet
1/4 cup or less milk
Blend well.

Super Berry Smoothie

by Jessy (VA)
1 Cup blueberries
1/2 Cup blackberries
1/2 Cup raspberries
1/2 Cup white grape juice
1 Cup strawberry yogurt
1/2 Cup ice cubes (optional)
Add all ingredients together in a blender and blend together until smooth.

Fruit Craze Smoothie

by Blair (USA)
1 Cup frozen strawberries
1/2 Cup fresh or frozen raspberries, blueberries, banana pieces
1/2 Cup milk
2 tbsp. sugar
Add ingredients together into the blender and blend until smooth.

Strawberry & Blueberry Deluxe Smoothie

Add about a cup of ice
1 1/2 Cups Milk
1/2 Cup blueberries
3 Strawberries
1 1/2 T. Sugar
Add all ingredients to blender and blend until ice cubes are crushed.

Purple Tummy Yummy

by Breanna (OK)
2 frozen bananas, skins removed and cut in chunks
1/2 Cup frozen blueberries
1 Cup orange juice
1 teaspoon honey(optional)
1 teaspoon vanilla extract (optional)
Add all ingredients to blender and blend until smooth.

Apple Smoothies

Apple and Ice

1 apple (sliced)
1 cup of ice
a splash of apple juice
Add all ingredients to blender and blend until ice cubes are crushed.

Apple Orange Smoothie

by Ryan
2 oranges, peeled and sectioned
1 apple, peeled and cut in slices
1/2 Cup orange juice
5 ice cubes
Add all ingredients to blender and blend until smooth.

Simple Banana and Apple Blast

1 apple, cored and sliced
1 banana, sliced
1 Cup natural yogurt
1/4 Cup milk
pinch of sugar
Add ingredients together in a blender and blend until smooth.

Healthy Fruit Smoothie Blend

by Jacque (California)
1/3 cup pineapple (plus juice)
1 cored and sliced apple
1 peeled frozen banana
5 fresh strawberries
1/2 Cup vanilla yogurt
1 scoop of any flavor protein powder
Blend until smooth.

Grape Smoothie

Grape and Strawberry

2 apples peeled and cut in slices
6 strawberries
a handful of grapes
1/2 cup ice cubes
Add all together and blend until smooth.

Grape Orange

1 Cup grapes
1 orange peeled and sliced
1 Cup frozen fruit
Blend until nice and smooth.

Coconut Smoothies

Jungle Smoothie

by Clarissa (North Carolina)
1 Cup coconut milk
1 half banana
1/2 Cup orange juice
1/4 Cup assorted berries
2 scoops vanilla yogurt or ice cream
Put milk and ice cream in blender for 1 minute. Add
banana, orange juice, and berries. Blend for 3 minutes.

Coconut Smoothie

by Sarah (England)
1/2 Cup coconut
1 Cup coconut milk
2 T. vanilla yogurt
1/2 Cup of crushed ice
Add all ingredients to blender and blend until ice cubes are
crushed.

Hawaii Coconut and Mango Smoothie

by Jayden (WI)
2 soft mangoes, peeled cut in pieces
2 soft coconuts peeled
1/2 Cup milk
4 ice cubes
Add all ingredients to blender and blend until ice cubes are
crushed.

Pincocoaya

by Cassie(Nanaimo)
2-3 pineapple slices
1 Cup coconut milk
1 papaya, cut in pieces
1 banana sliced
2 Cups of ice
1/2 Cup water
Blend together until desired thickness

Raspberry Smoothie

Banana Berry

1 banana, cut in slices
1 Cup milk
2 ice cubes
2 Cups frozen raspberries
Mix in blender until ice is crushed.

Super Berry Smoothie

2 Cups raspberries (fresh or frozen)
1/2 Cup milk
1 Cup orange juice
4 ice cubes
Blend thoroughly until smooth.

Mixed Berry

2 Cups frozen mixed berries
1 tsp of sugar
1 1/2 Cups milk
1 1/2 Cups yogurt (any flavor)
Put the mixed berries, milk, and yogurt in the blender.
Blend it together. When it is smooth add the sugar, then
blend it for another 15 seconds.

Banana Berry

2 Cups of orange juice
2 bananas

2 handfuls of raspberries
Blend together until smooth.

Very Berry

2 Cups raspberries or berries
1 Cup vanilla yogurt
2 teaspoons of sugar
1/2 Cup of ice (crushed or cubed)
Mix ingredients in a blender until smooth.

Kiwi Smoothies

Raspberry and Kiwi

2-3 Cups of sliced kiwi
2-3 Cups of raspberries
1 Cup of ice
1 Cup of any yogurt
Blend together and enjoy

Kiwi Strawberry Smoothie

by Jessica (CA)
5-8 Strawberries
4 kiwis (peeled and cut in half)
1 cup of milk
1 tablespoon vanilla
1/2 cup ice
Blend until smooth. Serves 2

Strawberry Kiwi

by DeAsarae (Indiana)
1 Cup of frozen strawberries
4 kiwi's, cut in pieces
2 Cups of any fruity drink
3/4 Cup of soy milk
Blend.

Fruit Blend Smoothie

1 Cup fresh strawberries
1 banana cut into pieces
2 Cups orange juice
a little over one cup of milk (2%)
1 kiwi skinned and cut into pieces
Blend until smooth.

Pineapple Smoothie

Tutti Frutti Smoothie

1/2 banana
4 strawberries
2 spoonfuls of frozen pineapple concentrate
1 mixed berry yogurt
a hint of vanilla
Blend until smooth.

Strawberry and "Pinana" Swoosh

by Alicia (Wisconsin)
2 Cups strawberries
1 Cup banana
1 can of pineapple with juice
8.5 oz of yogurt any flavor
Blend everything together except one cup strawberries and
4.25 oz of yogurt. After all is liquidated put aside. Take
your remaining yogurt and strawberries and mix them
together separately; mush the strawberries in. Pour in
smoothie mixture.

Pineapple Strawberry Banana

by Beth (Northumberland)
1/4 of pineapple juice carton
3 bananas
1 small carton plain yogurt
4-5 strawberries
2 tsp of honey (if needed to sweeten)
Blend together until smooth.

Banana Pineapple

by Brooke Ann (USA)
1 1/2 Cups of pineapple juice
2 Cups of chopped frozen banana
1/2 Cup vanilla yogurt
1/2 T. of honey
Place all ingredients in blender and process until smooth.

Apple Berry Pine Nana

by Kristen (CA)
1 Cup frozen strawberries
1/2 Cup frozen mixed berries
1/2 Cup frozen pineapple pieces
1 sliced and cored apple
1 peeled and sliced banana
1 Cup plain frozen yogurt
1 Cup orange juice
1/2 Cup milk
2 tablespoons sugar
Blend until smooth.

Banana, Coconut, and Pineapple

by Rainey (Ohio)
1-2 bananas, cut in slices
1/2 Cup of creamed coconut
1 Cup of crushed pineapple
3 Cups of ice
Add pineapple, bananas, coconut, then add ice gradually.
Blend till smooth.

Hawaiian Smoothie

by Jessica (CA)
1 can of dole pineapple
2 Cups of coconut milk
1 Cup of ice
1 Cup of orange juice
2 scoops of vanilla yogurt
Blend until smooth

Blackberry Smoothie

Berry Dream

by Natasha (Scotland)
2 Cups Strawberries(fresh or frozen)
1 Cup raspberries (fresh or frozen)
1 Cup blackberries (fresh or frozen)
4 or more ice cubes
Put in blender and blend until smooth

Berry Yogurt Smoothie

1 Cup raspberries, blackberries or strawberries
2 Tablespoons of vanilla yogurt
1 Cup orange juice
1 Cup milk
Put in blender and blend until smooth

Moolicious Berry Smoothie

by Mallika (Pennsylvania)
8-10 blackberries
1 banana, peeled and sliced
1 Cup 2% milk
1 teaspoon of sugar
Blend all ingredients together. Pour into glass and enjoy
with a purple straw !

Berry Blast

by Sintajah (Atlanta)
1 Cup strawberries, blackberries or raspberries
4-5 ice cubes
Place berries in blender or food processor with ice and let
blend on high or medium.
Let blend until completely processed. Stir and serve.

Yumberry smoothie

1/2 Cup blueberries
1/2 Cup blackberries
1/4 Cup strawberries
1 Cup milk
Blend and enjoy

Dessert Smoothies

Chocolate Smoothie

by Gwen (Illinois)
1/2 Cup chocolate chips
1 whole banana
1/2 Cup strawberries
1/2 Cup milk
Blend together. Put in a glass with whipped cream on top
and it is delicious! If you chose you can top the whip cream
with chocolate chips or M&M's.

Strawberry Banana Blitz

by Keira (Canada)
8 sliced strawberries
1 sliced banana
3 scoops of ice cream
1/2 cup milk
10 ice cubes
Add all ingredients to blender. Blend until smooth.

Lemonade smoothie

by Alyssa (buffalo)
2 tablespoons of lemon juice
3 ice cubes
2 teaspoons of sugar
1/2 cup of lemon or lemon meringue pie yogurt
blend for 20 seconds for your awesome lemony smoothie.

Banana Chocolate Smoothie

2 small bananas
2/3 Cup chocolate chips
2/3 Cup milk
1/2 Cup ice-cubes
1/4 Cup yogurt
Blend until smooth.

Jell-O Berry Smoothie

1/2 Cup milk (add more if flavor is too tangy)
1/2 cup strawberries
1/2 Cup ice cubes
1 Cup yogurt
1 Packet of Jell-O (My kids love the mixed berry Jell-O)
Add ingredients in blender and blend until smooth.

Banana Chocolate

4 ice cubes
2 spoons of vanilla yogurt
1 Cup of milk
1 banana
chocolate syrup
Blend until smooth. Drizzle top with chocolate syrup.

Banana Surprise

by Victoria (Canada)
2 Bananas
4 Strawberries
2 regular cups of yogurt, any flavor
2 regular cups of chocolate pudding bought in store.
OR
3 scoops of ice cream. Any flavor.

Banana Nesquick Smoothie

3/4 Cups milk
1/2 Cup ice
1/2 medium banana
1/4 Cup Orange Juice
3 Tbsp. strawberry nesquick powder mix.
Directions:
Put all ingredients in your blender and blend until smooth. I put more than 1/2 cup of ice to make it thicker. Pour into glasses and top with a scoop of ice cream or whip cream on top.

Pumpkin Milkshake

1/2 Cup pumpkin puree
3/4 Cup vanilla yogurt
1/2 Cup milk
1-2 scoops vanilla ice cream
1/4 teaspoon cinnamon
1/8 teaspoon nutmeg
Add all ingredients to blender. Blend until smooth.

Fruit Galore Smoothie

by Tucker (CA)
3 Scoops Vanilla Ice Cream
2 Scoops Strawberry Ice Cream
1/2 Cup orange juice
1/2 Cup crushed pineapple
4 maraschino cherries and 1 tbsp cherry juice
1/4 Cup milk
4 ice cubes
Blend together until ice is crushed.

Orange Milkshake

by Oscar (Australia)
1/2 Cup milk
1/2 Cup orange juice
5 tablespoons ice cream
Mix all in a blender.

Peanut Butter Smoothies

Peanut Butter and Chocolate Smoothie

by Patricia (Canada)
1 Cup milk
1 tbsp. peanut butter
1 tsp. chocolate syrup
1/4 very ripe banana *
2 or 3 ice cubes, depending on desired thickness
1 tsp. vanilla extract
* you can slice up very ripe bananas and put them in a
baggie or container beforehand and store in the freezer,
taking a slice out each time you want to make this recipe or
others containing bananas. It actually makes the smoothie
thicker and colder and the very ripe bananas add a healthy
dose of sweetness!

Elvis Smoothie

by Connor (MN)
1 frozen banana
1/4 Cup peanut butter
1/2 Cup vanilla yogurt
1/2 Cup milk
1 tsp honey
1/2 Cup crushed ice
Add all ingredients to blender. Blend until smooth.

Peanut Butter Banana

by Michele (Canada)
2 spoons of peanut butter
2 cups of milk
2 bananas peeled and chopped
1 spoon of chocolate syrup
2 1/2 cups of crushed ice
Mix all together in blender. Blend until smooth.

Chocolate Drizzle

by Keira (Canada)
1 sliced banana
1/4 Cup peanut butter
15 ice cubes
1 Cup milk
Blend until smooth and drizzle chocolate syrup on top of smoothie.

Peanut Butter Banana Smoothie

by Miyuki (El Paso TX)
1 banana, cut in two
spoonful of Peanut Butter
1 Cup Milk
1/2 Cup Ice
Mix ingredients together in a blender and blend until smooth.

5993247R00033

Printed in Great Britain
by Amazon.co.uk, Ltd.,
Marston Gate.